MUSIC MINISTRY UNPLUGGED

MUSIC MINISTRY UNPLUGGED

REAL LESSONS FOR THOSE WHO LEAD AND SERVE IN MUSIC MINISTRY

DR. WILL HARRIS

Published by J Merrill Publishing, Inc.
A division of J Merrill One
434 Hillpine Drive
Columbus, OH 43207
www.JMerrill.pub

Library of Congress Control Number: [PCN]

Paperback ISBN: 978-1-961475-72-4
eBook ISBN: 978-1-961475-73-1

Printed in the United States of America
First Edition

10 9 8 7 6 5 4 3 2 1

Portions of the editorial and publishing workflow may have been enhanced using proprietary AI systems developed by J Merrill One.

PROLOGUE

Music has always been at the heart of the Church's life. From the ancient psalms of Israel to the hymns of the early Church, and from the spirituals to the gospel music that have shaped African American worship, music has served as a powerful tool for theology, teaching, and transformation. It is more than melody and harmony—it is ministry. Church music leaders stand at a unique crossroads where art meets faith, and spiritual formation deepens through song. Leading a music ministry demands not only musical skill, but also spiritual maturity and cultural sensitivity.

It was a cold winter evening in Memphis, Tennessee, when I set out to begin a new chapter in ministry. I had just accepted the position of Minister of Music at Greater Lewis Street Baptist Church, on the corner of Poplar and East Parkway. Dressed in my best slacks and a freshly pressed shirt, I felt ready for battle. At twenty-three, brimming with energy and confidence, I believed myself fully prepared for the task ahead. After all, I'd been playing for churches since I was fourteen. Though Memphis was much larger than my hometown of Oxford, Mississippi, I assumed this would be a simple step forward.

During the interview, Deacon Charles Dickinson asked if I appreciated all styles of music. With certainty, I assured him I could handle any style he imagined.

At my first rehearsal, I met a seasoned musician who had served the church faithfully for years. She was all business—serious, skilled, and clearly unenthused about a young man, nearly young enough to be her great-grandson, stepping into the Minister of Music role.

Tension developed quickly. After a few rehearsals, she concluded I was not well-versed in traditional gospel music. I, in turn, dismissed her style, criticizing her for playing mostly in one key and making everything sound the same. Our disagreements soon overshadowed the music. Determined to prove myself, I relied on flashy organ runs and youthful pride.

What I failed to realize was that arrogance and self-absorption would not earn respect or strengthen the ministry. My immaturity, paired with her resistance, created more conflict than anyone expected. Matters escalated until the chairman of the deacons called us into a meeting. Frustrated, I told him: either she would have to go, or I would leave.

Looking back, I see God's hand in that moment. He knew the path He had set for me. Even in my immaturity, He was shaping me. My calling required pruning and growth—time spent under wise leaders, gaining new experiences, learning not just the art of music but the heart of ministry. Over the years, God has allowed me to grow, to serve, and to mentor others, helping them avoid some of the same mistakes I made as a young musician.

This book is born out of that journey. Music Ministry Unplugged is meant to enlighten, educate, edify, and support those who lead and serve in music and fine arts ministries in the local church. My prayer is that as you read, you'll find both joy and knowledge—practical tools to strengthen your ministry, and inspiration from my own experiences. May this resource guide you not only in the work of music, but in the greater work of ministry itself.

1

THE CALLING

Our world offers countless career paths. Many pursue professions for money, status, or reputation—spending years in study and training, hoping to land a role that brings happiness and fulfillment. My journey began similarly. I dreamed of becoming an educator, so I earned a degree in music, taught in the Memphis school system, and later completed a master's in teacher leadership. My goal was to one day chair a high school fine arts department or teach in higher education.

But God had a different plan.

Eventually, I left the classroom for full-time ministry. At first, I wondered, "Lord, why am I here?" Over time, I realized that what I had longed to do in academia—teaching, training, equipping —I was now called to do in the church. The Holy Spirit whispered, "Everything you hoped to do in academia, you can do here. Teach and train my people."

That moment of clarity transformed my career into a calling.

Scripture reminds us: "You did not choose me, but I chose you and appointed you so that you might go and bear fruit" (John 15:16). Serving in music ministry is not just work—it's a divine assignment that shapes lives and builds God's kingdom.

REQUIREMENTS OF THE CALL

The role of a minister or director of music is unique. Music is one of ministry's most powerful tools because it connects with everyone on some level. Not all can sing or play, but everyone responds to music. In worship, music retells God's story and prepares hearts for His Word.

For the African American church, music is inseparable from worship. It stirs faith, strengthens believers, and offers youth a positive, formative outlet. Music ministry is more than performance—it's discipleship, service, and pastoral care.

This calling requires more than skill; it requires the heart of Jesus. Week after week, choir members and musicians arrive for rehearsal, often carrying burdens unseen—financial struggles, grief, family challenges. Music becomes more than practice; it becomes healing. A well-led rehearsal can encourage weary souls and remind them of God's presence.

To serve faithfully, a leader must embody four qualities: strength, wisdom, empathy, and compassion.

STRENGTH

Rehearsals are demanding. A two-hour practice can feel like twelve. Directors must balance creativity with discipline, drawing out the best from singers through repetition, nuance, and careful instruction—leaving all involved exhausted. Strength—physical, emotional, and spiritual—is essential.

> *"The Lord is my strength and my shield; my heart trusts in him, and he helps me"*
>
> — PSALM 28:7

Pray for Strength

Heavenly Father, You are our refuge and strength, an ever-present help in need. As I lead others in worship, give me endurance when the work feels overwhelming. Strengthen me for long rehearsals and remind me that we are preparing hearts to encounter You. Fill me with joy and perseverance as I serve. In Jesus' name, Amen.

WISDOM

Great leaders read the room. Sometimes, no words are needed—you sense the atmosphere. Some rehearsals require discipline; others call for a pause, encouragement, or even spontaneous worship. This discernment comes with prayer and practice.

> *"If any of you lacks wisdom, you should ask God, who gives*

> *generously to all without finding fault, and it will be given to you"*
>
> — JAMES 1:5

Pray for Wisdom

Lord, You are the source of all wisdom. Help me discern the needs of those I lead. Give me the right words, songs, and timing so that each rehearsal becomes more than practice—it becomes ministry. Guide me to lead with understanding and grace. In Jesus' name, Amen.

EMPATHY

Before leading with your gifts, lead with your heart. Servanthood comes first. Choir members need to know their leader genuinely cares—not just about their voices, but their lives. Are you praying for them? Do you know their burdens? Do you understand how a lyric might impact their hearts? Empathy opens doors for deeper ministry.

> *"Carry each other's burdens, and in this way you will fulfill the law of Christ"*

— GALATIANS 6:2

Pray for Empathy

Gracious God, give me a servant's heart. Help me see beyond the music to the person, and beyond the performance to the need. Teach me to walk with those I lead in both joy and sorrow, and to care for their souls as much as their songs. In Jesus' name, Amen.

COMPASSION

Empathy feels, but compassion acts. Compassionate leaders go beyond understanding to practical care—through prayer, encouragement, or tangible help. Compassion makes Christ's love visible.

> *"Be kind and compassionate to one another, forgiving each other, just as in Christ God forgave you"*
>
> — EPHESIANS 4:32

Pray for Compassion

Loving Father, fill me with compassion that moves me to action. Help me to be Your hands and feet to those who are hurting. May our ministry be known not just for music but for love expressed in real and practical ways. In Jesus' name, Amen.

Serving in music ministry is not just about leading songs—it's about answering a call. It is hard work, but it is holy work. It requires strength, wisdom, empathy, and compassion, grounded in scripture and fueled by the Spirit. When we fully embrace this calling, we discover a peace and joy that no paycheck or title can match.

> *"Whatever you do, work at it with all your heart, as working for the Lord, not for human masters"*
>
> — COLOSSIANS 3:23

There is no greater privilege than serving God by serving His people through the gift of music.

2

DISCOVERING GIFTS AND TALENTS IN YOUR MINISTRY

Many years ago, during a church interview, I was asked a question that completely caught me off guard. The interviewer, a former educator, presented this scenario:

> I have been singing in the choir for years. I am an amazing soloist, but no one knows. Discover me!

How do you answer that? I was baffled at the time, but the question stayed with me. It highlights one of the greatest challenges in music ministry: uncovering gifts that are hidden, overlooked, or underdeveloped within your congregation.

Finding and nurturing artistic gifts in your ministry is no small task. Over the years, I've noticed a few "types" of gifts that directors frequently encounter:

1. **The Enthusiastic Volunteer**

This is the singer who loves music but doesn't quite have the skill to match their passion. They sing with all their heart—sometimes with all the wrong notes. Some are even tone-deaf and don't realize it.

Here's where wisdom and creativity come in. Your job isn't to crush their spirit but to help them blend with others in a way that contributes positively to the choir. Scripture tells us to "make a joyful noise unto the Lord." One person's joyful noise may not sound joyful to the human ear, but turning anyone away from worship is never the answer. Sometimes your role is to encourage, shape, and lovingly direct so their "noise" becomes part of a greater harmony.

Leadership Tip: Always value willingness before talent. A teachable spirit can grow; a proud spirit cannot.

2. The Talented but Hesitant Singer

This singer has all the skill in the world, but you nearly have to beg them to take a solo. They either lack confidence or always have a reason why the song you've assigned "just won't work."

The key here is relationship. They need to know you see their gift, understand their voice, and believe in them. Sometimes they just need a gentle push. Other times, ego is involved—even in church choirs. In those cases, a little encouragement (and sometimes ego-stroking) gets them moving. Your job is to discern the real issue and help them reach their highest potential.

Leadership Tip: Never assign a task unless you're ready to support them through it. Confidence grows when singers know their leader won't let them fail.

3. The "I Know My Part" Singer

This one can be tricky. They're decent singers, can hold their notes, but don't want to be pushed beyond "average." They'll say, "I listen to the radio. I know this song already. I don't need rehearsal."

But listening to the radio isn't the same as preparing for ministry. Rehearsal is about more than notes—it's about blending, dynamics, timing, and unity. This singer needs to be reminded that excellence is not optional in worship—it's required.

Their definition of "excellence" may differ from yours. They might think skipping rehearsals but showing up to sing is good enough. For this type, you'll need to be firm: set clear rules for participation, emphasize the importance of showing up, and model the excellence you expect.

Leadership Tip: Excellence isn't perfection—it's consistency. Set standards and hold everyone (including yourself) accountable.

THE BIGGER PICTURE

Every music director's job is to take these different personalities, abilities, and levels of commitment and shape them into one unified sound that glorifies God. It's like cooking: strong flavors, bland ingredients, and a few things that might taste strange on their own—but together, the result can be amazing.

Questions for Reflection

- How are you discovering gifts and talents in your congregation?
- Are there singers in your pews who aren't in the choir yet?
- Are there poets, spoken word artists, or instrumentalists who could add to your worship experience?

Gifts aren't always obvious. Sometimes people are waiting—just like that interview scenario—for someone to discover them. As leaders, we must be intentional about truly learning our congregations. Your role isn't just to direct music—it's to direct people into the fullness of their gifts.

3

SELECTING APPROPRIATE MUSIC FOR WORSHIP

The ministry of music is more than picking songs people enjoy—it's about shaping the worship life of a congregation. Scripture says, "Sing to the Lord a new song; sing to the Lord, all the earth. Sing to the Lord, bless his name; tell of his salvation from day to day" (Psalm 96:1–2). Music is a vital way we proclaim God's story. When word and song are thoughtfully brought together, worship becomes more than a collection of parts—it becomes a unified experience that helps people see and celebrate God's goodness.

THE VALUE OF PLANNING

Some churches shy away from planning, fearing it might stifle the Spirit. Yet Paul reminds us, "God is not a God of disorder but of peace" (1 Corinthians 14:33). Planning doesn't push the Spirit out—it actually creates space for the Spirit to work with greater clarity and focus. When a service is well-planned, the sermon, scripture, and songs flow together, guiding the congregation into a deeper encounter with God.

Robert Webber wrote, "Worship is a rehearsal of God's story of redemption. When word and song come together in unity, they form the narrative by which the church remembers who it is and to whom it belongs" (*Worship Is a Verb*). Good planning doesn't make worship rigid; it helps tell the story more clearly.

PRINCIPLES FOR SELECTING WORSHIP MUSIC

1. **Remember Your Church's Story**

Ecclesiastes teaches, "For everything there is a season, and a time for every matter under heaven"

(Ecclesiastes 3:1). Every church has its own history and traditions. Respecting that legacy is important, but so is listening for God's vision for the future. Strive for balance: include the songs that shaped your church in the past while also introducing new music that can carry the congregation forward.

2. **Learn Your Congregation's Worship Voice**

Every congregation has a unique "worship voice." Some connect deeply with hymns, others with gospel or contemporary worship, and many with a blend. Pay attention to what resonates with your people. Paul modeled this sensitivity: "I have become all things to all people, that by all means I might save some" (1 Corinthians 9:22). The goal isn't to please everyone, but to lead in ways that fit your church's identity.

3. **Make Sure the Songs Line Up with Scripture**

Colossians 3:16 urges us to "let the word of Christ dwell in you richly... singing psalms and hymns and spiritual songs." Our songs should proclaim something true about God. If a song can't be tied back to scripture, it likely doesn't belong in worship. Even "inspirational" songs should point us to God's truth.

4. Pay Attention to the Calendar—Both Church and World

The church year—Advent, Christmas, Lent, Easter, Pentecost—connects us to God's grand story. At the same time, people live by the "regular" calendar—school years, holidays, and even moments of crisis. Good worship leaders are aware of both. Romans 12:15 reminds us, "Rejoice with those who rejoice, weep with those who weep." Song choices should reflect both eternal truths and what our people are experiencing week by week.

Choosing music for worship is a holy responsibility. It's not about filling time or matching styles; it's about proclaiming the gospel, shaping faith, and caring for people through song. When worship leaders plan with both scripture and sensitivity, music becomes more than performance—it becomes ministry. As Robert

Webber reminds us, worship is where the church rehearses God's story. Our job is to choose songs that help the church remember—and live out—that story in the world.

4

THE PASTOR AND MINISTER OF MUSIC DYNAMIC

This relationship forms the backbone of most churches and their worship experiences. Because word and music are the dominant elements in worship—especially in the African American church—these two roles are vital to the spiritual health and vitality of the congregation. The Pastor's vision should help shape the direction of the music and arts ministry, creating a unified expression of worship that glorifies God and edifies the body of Christ.

Often, the Minister of Music isn't seminary-trained, and the Pastor may not have a music background. Collaboration isn't just beneficial—it's necessary for a Spirit-led worship experience. As Scripture reminds us, "Two are better than one, because they have a good return for their labor" (Ecclesiastes 4:9, NIV). Each leader brings unique gifts and perspectives; together, they create something far greater than either could alone.

THE NEED FOR INTENTIONAL CULTIVATION

This relationship requires intentional attention and nurturing. Even with a strong spiritual calling, we must remember our humanity. Paul's words in Philippians 2:3–4 are a guiding principle: "Do nothing out of selfish ambition or vain conceit. Rather, in humility value others above yourselves... not looking to your own interests but each of you to the interests of the others" (NIV).

Challenges will arise—egos, control, jealousy, intimidation, and more—that can threaten unity. As a Music Director, I remind myself daily: I ultimately answer to God, and then to the shepherd God has placed to lead the ministry.

THE FOUNDATION: MUTUAL RESPECT

Respect must be the cornerstone. Each person

must respect the role, calling, and gift that God has placed in the other.

- **Respect for the Role:** Both Pastor and Minister of Music hold God-ordained positions. "But in fact God has placed the parts in the body, every one of them, just as he wanted them to be" (1 Corinthians 12:18, NIV).
- **Respect for the Calling:** Each leader is specifically called and equipped by God. "God's gifts and his call are irrevocable" (Romans 11:29, NIV). Dishonoring another's calling is questioning God's wisdom.
- **Respect for the Gift:** The talents and abilities each brings are divine endowments for building up the church. "Each of you should use whatever gift you have received to serve others, as faithful stewards of God's grace..." (1 Peter 4:10, NIV).

When both Pastor and Minister of Music operate from mutual respect, honoring God's assignments, unity flourishes and God's presence is manifest. In this unity, blessings flow, transforming worship from performance into authentic encounter.

BUILDING, UNDERSTANDING, AND EMBRACING THE VISION

Each leader has a vision that should be shared. The Minister of Music isn't just responsible for teaching music—they curate an atmosphere for worship. Ask: What is your leader's vision? What is their style? How do they view worship? How can you work together to marry word and music in ways that are refreshing, renewing, and innovative?

Music leaders must clearly understand the Pastor's vision to carry it out effectively. Since neither may be an expert in the other's field, developing a collaborative vision is often most helpful.

MUTUAL RESPECT IN PRACTICE

I'll never forget a conversation with a Caucasian pastor who asked, "How is Leonard doing?" I was momentarily confused—he was referring to the Pastor I served with at the time. I realized then that I'd never even considered my Pastor's first name. My reverence was so great, I never thought to use it.

A healthy respect for your leader is essential. But there's a difference between respect and reverence —between honoring a position and placing someone on a pedestal. When that line blurs, the relationship strains, and partnership becomes stressful.

The temptation to elevate spiritual leaders beyond their humanity is real. But Pastors are human— they have bad days, make mistakes, and carry their own insecurities. Placing them on a pedestal does a disservice to them and to ourselves.

For the Minister of Music, this dynamic is especially complex: your boss is also your spiritual leader. This dual relationship can create unique pressure—wanting to please, fearing creative choices might offend, or worrying that disagreement equals rebellion.

WALKING ON EGGSHELLS

When you begin walking on eggshells around your Pastor, something precious is lost. Creativity dims, the courage to offer perspective vanishes, and authenticity is buried under anxiety and people-pleasing.

You may second-guess every decision: Should I suggest this new song? Will sharing concerns seem uncommitted? This isn't just about feelings or workplace discomfort. When fear silences your voice, the congregation loses the full benefit of your calling.

THE SOLUTION

If you're in an unhealthy dynamic, start with honest self-reflection. Have you contributed to the pedestal problem by withholding your voice? Have you assumed the worst without talking it through?

Prayerfully consider initiating a conversation—not from accusation or frustration, but from a desire for a healthier partnership.

Remember, taking your leader off the pedestal isn't disrespect. It's seeing them clearly, honoring their humanity, and creating space for authentic partnership. That's better for you, your Pastor, and —most importantly—the people you're both called to serve.

5

EMPLOYING MUSICIANS AND MUSIC STAFF – THE ROLE OF MUSICIANS IN WORSHIP

EMPLOYING MUSICIANS

In my early years as a Minister of Music, my requirements for music staff were simple: be skilled and be saved. I remember a musician once asking, "How do I know if I'm saved?" I explained Romans 10:9 and asked if he believed. He confessed his faith that very day.

Too often, churches hire musicians who are talented but not spiritually connected. It's not enough to have a passion for music—musicians must connect with the ministry's vision. Technical ability without spiritual alignment creates a disconnect that the congregation can sense.

QUALIFICATIONS: SKILLS VS. REQUIREMENTS

When hiring music staff, seek those who are both skilled and qualified. But what does "qualified" mean in your context? Some musicians have degrees but struggle to play by ear; others excel by ear but can't read music. Leaders must decide what's practical for their worship setting. Ideally, a team would have both strengths.

Many churches require music degrees and reading skills in job descriptions, yet never open a hymnal —instead, lyrics are projected on screens. If your choir learns songs by rote and hymn singing is rare, is reading music truly necessary?

Ask yourself: Does your church sing anthems or spirituals that require sheet music? If not, reconsider whether reading music is essential. Don't impose requirements that don't serve your ministry's real needs.

THE ROLE OF INSTRUMENTAL MUSIC IN WORSHIP

Practically, musicians accompany choirs or singers, but their role is much broader. In

Scripture, David played skillfully and drove out evil spirits from Saul (1 Samuel 16:23). Musicians who are anointed and spiritually connected can shift the worship atmosphere as powerfully as singers. Instrumental music should never be reduced to background—it is a vital part of worship.

UNDERSTANDING THE MUSICIAN'S ROLE IN AFRICAN AMERICAN WORSHIP

Hiring musicians and helping them understand their role in worship is crucial. African American churches often have spontaneous moments requiring flexibility and creativity. Musicians must be prepared for planned selections and able to flow with the Spirit during worship.

This art form is often caught, not just taught. Flowing in worship comes from years of improvisation, observation, and mentorship in the Black church tradition.

Providing instrumental music during the sermon is an art highly valued in the African American church. For some, it comes naturally; for others, it brings anxiety. This moment demands skill, attention, and sensitivity—reading the preacher's cues and sensing the direction of the Spirit. It often leads to extending the invitation for someone to accept Christ.

BEYOND THE GIFT: DISCIPLESHIP AND DEVELOPMENT

Many musicians feel they're valued only for their talent, not as whole people. Leaders must mentor, develop, and disciple musicians—investing in their spiritual growth as well as their technical skills.

Musicians need spiritual formation, understanding of theology, and the heart behind worship. When they feel valued as members of the body, their ministry becomes transformative.

Finally, leaders must ensure that musicians have a heart for God and sensitivity to the worship atmosphere. Instrumentalists are invaluable—their spiritual attentiveness can make the difference between a technically correct service and a truly anointed worship experience.

6

EMPLOYING MUSIC STAFF, ADDITIONAL SINGERS, AND CHOIR DIRECTORS

When bringing on music staff and additional singers, the same core principles apply: Are they skilled, and are they saved? In my experience, discernment is crucial. Someone may be a talented vocalist or choir director, but do they have your best interest at heart? Are they fully on board with your leadership? Are they seeking a platform for themselves, or are they truly committed to advancing the ministry?

Credentials and experience matter, but they are not everything. You might hire someone with impressive credentials, but do they have a heart for God? How much practical ministry experience do they bring? Can they navigate the unique dynamics of church ministry?

It's vital that everyone understands their role in assisting the Minister of Music. Avoid gray areas—unclear expectations and undefined boundaries can create serious issues. Clear communication from the start prevents confusion, competition, and conflict.

BUILDING A MUSIC TEAM WITH HEART AND SKILL

Hiring musicians and staff is more than filling positions—it's about building a ministry team that leads God's people into authentic worship. The most effective music ministries prioritize both spiritual connection and musical excellence, refusing to settle for one without the other.

As you build your team, keep these principles in mind:

- **Spiritual alignment matters most.** A technically proficient musician who is spiritually disconnected cannot facilitate true worship. A musician with a heart for

God, who is willing to grow, can become invaluable.

- **Context determines qualifications.** Don't impose requirements that don't serve your ministry's real needs. Be honest about what your worship context requires, and hire accordingly.
- **Discipleship is essential.** Musicians are not just service providers—they are ministers. Invest in their spiritual growth, mentor them, and help them see their role as a calling, not just a job.
- **Discernment protects the ministry.** Pay attention to motives, attitudes, and alignment. Skills can be developed, but character issues or misaligned hearts can undermine everything you're building.
- **Clear expectations prevent conflict.** Define roles, set boundaries, and communicate openly. When everyone knows their lane and the overall vision, the ministry flourishes.

The musicians and staff you hire will shape your church's worship culture for years to come. Take time to pray, seek wisdom, and build a team that honors God with both their gifts and their hearts.

When skill and spirituality unite under anointed leadership, worship becomes transformative—not only for the congregation, but for the musicians themselves.

Remember Psalm 33:3: "Sing to him a new song; play skillfully, and shout for joy." Both matter—the skillful playing and the joyful heart behind it. May your music ministry embody both as you lead God's people in worship.

7

THE ROLE OF THE PSALMIST

In 2 Chronicles 20, we encounter a remarkable story: King Jehoshaphat, facing battle against the Moabites and Ammonites, appoints men to sing and praise God at the front of the army. As they began to sing and give praise, the Lord set ambushes against their enemies, leading to victory.

This story offers a powerful glimpse into the role of the psalmist—those who stand on the front line each time the church gathers to minister through music. Every worship experience matters and should never be taken lightly. When we minister, we stand at the forefront of spiritual battle, ushering in God's presence and cultivating an atmosphere for worship. Music is a universal language, and to be used as a conduit for leading others into God's presence is an extreme honor.

For many, the corporate gathering is a source of refreshment and encouragement—sometimes the uplift needed just to make it through the week. For others, it may be their first encounter with worship, or a moment of refuge in a season of brokenness. As psalmists, we cannot afford to fumble this opportunity.

Yet we must acknowledge a vital truth: those who minister are often broken themselves, fighting to survive another day. Having the gift of music doesn't mean you're not struggling. God chooses and uses whom He desires. Scripture teaches that gifts come without repentance—God does not take back what He has given, even in our struggles. The gift of music is not just for others' encouragement; it's also a source of healing and strength for yourself.

The psalmist's role is both a privilege and a sacred responsibility. Like the singers before Jehoshaphat's army, we go ahead of the congregation, preparing the way for an encounter with God. This calling is not to be taken lightly. Through worship, lives are changed, hearts are healed, and spiritual battles are won.

In our humanity, we must remember that God uses broken vessels. Your struggles do not disqualify you—they often deepen your ministry and make your worship more authentic. As you stand on the front line week after week, minister to yourself with the same gift God has given you to minister to others. Let the songs that bring healing to the congregation bring healing to your own soul.

The psalmist's call is to be faithful, prepared, and surrendered. Embracing this calling with excellence and authenticity makes you part of a divine strategy—where praise becomes warfare, music ushers in victory, and broken people encounter a God who restores. Stand confidently on the front line, knowing that what you carry has the power to change lives—including your own.

8

CURATING MEANINGFUL MOMENTS IN WORSHIP

Many American congregations are now beautifully multi-ethnic and multi-generational. Engaging worshippers with diverse, faith-based music is essential for a well-balanced, biblical worship experience. Worship should reflect the unique climate of each church community—diverse and inclusive, never static.

Culture, socio-economic status, and countless other factors shape our worship preferences. Because culture is always evolving, there's no single worship style that satisfies everyone. Worship leaders must avoid complacency, consistently evaluating how to diversify music and create blended worship experiences.

Understanding the unique makeup of your congregation helps you select songs that foster unity and deepen engagement.

CREATIVE SCRIPTURE PRESENTATION

One long day at the Robert Webber Institute for Worship Studies, after orientation, tours, and dinner, I attended the Opening Convocation. The processional was formal, with pipe organ, brass, and the IWS Choir leading "The First Noel." Despite my exhaustion, I was drawn into worship alongside classmates from around the world.

Then came a scripture presentation unlike anything I'd seen. The reading centered on Moses and the burning bush. The narrator's delivery, paired with a choir blending mystical harmonies, transported me into the biblical scene. Suddenly, I saw how creative scripture presentation could transform worship and spark new passion in my own ministry.

Before this, I'd viewed dramatic arts as mere entertainment. I hadn't considered storytelling through scripture as a worship tool. Yet, the public reading of scripture has deep roots in Christian tradition. Justin Martyr described scripture readings in early worship, and Pliny's letter recounts believers singing hymns antiphonally to Christ.

Have you considered creative scripture presentation in your ministry? Could your dance ministry interpret scripture through movement? Could you pair scripture reading with instrumental music? These approaches can turn familiar texts into fresh encounters with God's Word.

THE PSALMS

"Psalm" comes from the Greek psalmos, meaning hymn of praise. The Psalms, written by authors like Moses, David, and Solomon, have served as daily devotionals and worship resources for centuries. Singing psalms in worship dates back to Exodus and the liberation from Egypt.

At IWS, I learned to present a Psalm as a spoken or sung response to scripture. My group paired Psalm 150 with a passage from Ephesians. Initially, it seemed odd, but Dr. Cherry's *The Worship Architect* clarified that worship is a conversation—revelation and response, not performance or passive listening. Corporate response through the Psalms brings worshippers into active engagement with God's Word.

As a worship leader, consider how you can incorporate Psalms more frequently, allowing the congregation to respond creatively and corporately.

EMBRACING THE LITURGICAL CALENDAR

There are many ways to curate significant moments in worship. Special days—Pentecost, Advent, Maundy Thursday—offer opportunities for creative, memorable experiences. For many, these days are unfamiliar. Use visual elements, teaching moments, or preparatory materials to help your congregation understand the richness of the Christian calendar.

Curating meaningful worship is both an art and a calling. It requires intentionality, creativity, and a deep commitment to serving a diverse body of believers. The transformative moment I experienced at IWS reminded me that worship is about encounter, not entertainment. When we step beyond our comfort zones and explore new expressions, we create spaces for God to meet His people in powerful ways.

As worship leaders, we are curators—selecting, arranging, and presenting elements that facilitate genuine encounters with God. This requires knowing your congregation: their cultures, generations, and spiritual hungers. Remain a student of both Scripture and culture, always learning how people connect with God.

Most importantly, remember that worship is a dialogue—a divine conversation of revelation and response. Dramatic scripture presentations, sung Psalms, and marking sacred seasons invite people into this holy conversation. Our task is to teach participation, not just attendance.

The worship experiences we create will shape faith for generations. Approach this sacred work with courage, creativity, and conviction. Dare to try new things, recover ancient practices, and blend diverse expressions into a tapestry that honors the unity and diversity of Christ's body. In doing so, we create not just services, but sacred moments—

times when heaven touches earth and lives are transformed.

May we always be amazed by the privilege of leading others into God's presence. And may the worship we curate point beyond ourselves to the One who alone is worthy of praise.

9

THE SOUND OF WORSHIP

A few years ago, I was invited to conduct a workshop at Mount Carmel Baptist Church in Indianapolis, IN. The theme, "The Sound of Worship," led me to discuss vocal sounds, the color of sounds, and how different sounds set the tone for various moods and modes in worship. This topic fascinated me.

Close your eyes for a moment and listen. What do you hear? Maybe it's traffic, the rustle of pages, or your own breathing. Sound is everywhere, shaping our experiences and emotions—often without us realizing it. Now imagine entering a worship space. Before you see the sanctuary or read the bulletin, you hear: the prelude, conversations, tuning instruments, anticipation in the air. Sound prepares us, moves us, and shapes how we encounter God.

WHAT IS WORSHIP?

Before understanding the sound of worship, we must understand worship itself. At its core, worship is showing reverence and adoration to God. Too often, congregations become audiences —evaluating performances, recording on phones, rather than participating in worship. True worship is active; it's something we do, not something done for us. This shift transforms how we approach worship and the sounds that accompany it.

WHAT DOES WORSHIP DO?

Effective worship accomplishes three essential movements—the three Rs: it Rehearses, Reflects, and Responds to God's story.

- **Rehearse:** Worship is remembrance. We recall God's goodness, mercy, justice, and truth—not because God needs reminding, but because we do.
- **Reflect:** Worship prompts personal introspection. We hold God's story up like

a mirror—how has God been faithful to me? Where do I need to align more closely with His truth?
- **Respond:** Worship doesn't end with the benediction. After rehearsing and reflecting, we're compelled to act—to share Christ and live out our faith daily. Worship leads to transformation beyond the sanctuary.

These movements—rehearsing, reflecting, and responding—form the framework for all worship expressions. Sound plays a crucial role in each.

THE SOUND OF WORSHIP: A THEOLOGICAL FOUNDATION

Psalm 33:3 says, "Sing to him a new song; play skillfully, and shout for joy." This single verse encompasses singing, instrumental skill, and vocal exclamation. The diversity of sound is intentional, reflecting God's design for worship.

THE ORIGIN OF SOUND

Before there was sight, there was sound. In Genesis 1:3, God spoke, "Let there be light." Sound

—God's spoken word—preceded the visible universe. Sound was God's creative instrument, the means through which everything came to be.

God's world is filled with diverse sounds: birds at dawn, ocean waves, insects buzzing, wind in the trees. This variety reflects a God who values beauty and intentionality. Humans alone have the capacity for complex speech, song, and intentional sound-making. We don't just make noise—we craft melodies, harmonies, and rhythms. We tell stories and express emotions words alone cannot capture. This ability mirrors our creation in God's image; the God who spoke creation into existence invites us to participate through the sounds we make in worship.

THE ART OF SINGING IN WORSHIP

Singing is the most universal worship expression. The human voice is remarkably versatile; different techniques evoke different emotions. Straight-tone singing is pure and direct; vibrato adds warmth and emotional depth. Dynamics matter—a whispered phrase draws focus, a full choir fills the sanctuary with majesty. Crescendos build anticipation, decrescendos create intimacy.

A phrase like "We give you all the glory" can be sung with straight tone for solemnity or with vibrato for warmth and expression. Neither is wrong—each serves a different worship moment and evokes a unique response to God.

THE SOUND OF SILENCE

In contemporary worship, we often fear silence, rushing to fill every moment. But silence creates space for reflection, for listening, for God's still small voice. Effective worship leadership knows when to sing and when to be still, when to play and when to pause.

THE VOICE OF INSTRUMENTS

Each instrument brings unique character to worship:

- **Strings:** Violins, cellos, and guitars create intimacy and contemplation with sustained, warm tones.
- **Winds:** Flutes, clarinets, and saxophones require breath, symbolizing the Spirit's movement. Their flow represents God's continuous presence.

- **Percussion:** Provides rhythm and energy, establishing the heartbeat of worship. Percussion can communicate celebration, urgency, or spiritual authority.

COLORS OF SOUND: MAJOR AND MINOR TONALITIES

Just as painters use colors to evoke emotions, worship leaders use tonalities. Major keys evoke joy, triumph, and celebration. Minor keys communicate depth, longing, or sorrow. A service that only uses major keys may feel superficial, missing the congregation's real struggles.

Sounds That Shape Worship Moments

Different moments call for different sounds:

- **Celebration:** Uptempo, percussion-heavy, bright timbres—trumpets, drums, soaring voices—invite rejoicing and physical response.
- **Warfare:** Bold, rhythmic, declarative—trumpet calls, driving percussion—proclaim God's power and our faith.
- **Intimate Worship:** Gentle vocals and

instrumentation, close-mic singing—invite personal reflection and prayer.
- **Silence:** Intentional quiet for listening and absorbing.
- **Transitions:** Smooth musical bridges move the congregation between moments, requiring skill and sensitivity.

As you plan worship, ask: What emotions does this sound evoke? What moment does it prepare for? How will the congregation respond? The goal isn't to manipulate emotions, but to create authentic spaces where people genuinely encounter God.

10

BUILDING AND MAINTAINING AN EFFECTIVE MUSIC AND ARTS MINISTRY

DEFINING EFFECTIVENESS IN YOUR MINISTRY

Before we can build or maintain an effective music ministry, we must first ask ourselves a fundamental question: What does "effective" actually mean for our ministry? The dictionary defines effective as being "successful in producing a desired or intended result." This simple definition carries profound implications for how we approach ministry leadership. Effectiveness is not measured by someone else's standards or by comparing ourselves to the church down the street. Rather, effectiveness is determined by whether we are achieving what

God has called us to accomplish in our unique context.

This brings us to a crucial principle that must guide everything we do in ministry.

THE PRINCIPLE OF INTENTION

Oprah Winfrey once said, "The intention for which you serve will ultimately determine your outcome." These words ring especially true in ministry. Our intentions shape our actions, our decisions, and ultimately, the fruit of our labor. If we serve with the intention of building our own reputation, we will make decisions that elevate ourselves. If we serve with the intention of pleasing people, we will constantly shift with the changing winds of opinion. But if we serve with the pure intention of glorifying God and edifying His people, our ministry will bear fruit that lasts.

Take a moment to reflect: What is your intention? Why did you accept the call to lead a music ministry? Is it to showcase talent, to create beautiful experiences, to build community, to usher people into God's presence, or perhaps a combination of these? Your honest answer to this question will set the course for everything that follows. Write it down. Pray over it. Return to it regularly, because your intention will be tested, and you'll need to remember why you started.

BUILDING YOUR MUSIC MINISTRY

Create, Share, and Cast the Vision

The foundation of any effective ministry is vision. Scripture reminds us in Proverbs 29:18 that "without a vision the people perish." A music ministry without clear vision is like a ship without a rudder—it may float, but it will never reach its intended destination. Vision provides direction, creates unity, and inspires commitment. It answers the question: Where is God leading us, and what will it look like when we get there?

Brainstorm Ways for Your Ministry to Be Effective

Creating vision begins with seeking God's heart for your ministry. Set aside time to pray, listen, and dream about what your music and arts ministry could become. What are the needs in your congregation? What gifts and talents has God placed within your ministry? What unique contribution can your ministry make to the life of your church and community?

During this brainstorming phase, don't limit yourself. Consider questions like: How can our ministry help people encounter God? How can we serve the broader church community? What would it look like if every person in our ministry was operating in their gifts? How can we develop emerging talent? What impact could we have beyond Sunday morning services? Write down every idea, even the ones that seem impossible. God specializes in the impossible.

Share This Vision with Your Pastor

Once you've begun to clarify the vision, your next critical step is to share it with your pastor. This isn't merely a courtesy—it's important for alignment and support. Your pastor carries the overall vision for the church, and your music ministry vision must fit within and support that larger purpose. Schedule time to sit down with your pastor and present your ideas. Listen to their feedback, ask questions, and be willing to adjust. This conversation will strengthen your vision and ensure that you have pastoral covering and support for what you're building.

Cast the Vision to Your Entire Music Ministry

After aligning with pastoral leadership, it's time to cast the vision to your entire music ministry. This is more than just announcing plans—it's about inspiring people to see what you see and inviting them to be part of something greater than themselves. Use creative ways to communicate the vision: share it during rehearsals, create visual presentations, tell stories that illustrate where you're going, and most importantly, connect the vision to each person's role and contribution.

When people understand the "why" behind what they're doing, they move from mere participation to passionate engagement. They're no longer just singing songs; they're partnering with God to transform lives through worship.

Execute the Vision

Vision without execution remains just a dream. Once you've cast the vision, develop a concrete plan to bring it to life. Break down the big vision into actionable steps with timelines and responsible parties. Create measurable goals that allow you to track progress. Celebrate small wins along the way. Remember that vision execution is a marathon, not a sprint. Stay committed even when enthusiasm wanes or obstacles arise. Keep reminding your team of where you're going and why it matters.

Administration, Organization, and Roles

A vision without structure will eventually collapse under its own weight. Clear organization and defined roles create the framework that allows your ministry to function smoothly and sustainably. When everyone knows their role and responsibilities, confusion decreases and effectiveness increases.

THE ROLE OF THE MINISTER OF MUSIC

As the Minister of Music, you are both a spiritual leader and an administrative manager. Spiritually, you set the tone for worship, model a heart of devotion, and shepherd the souls entrusted to your care. You're responsible for selecting music that edifies the congregation, preparing your team spiritually and musically, and creating an atmosphere where God's presence can be experienced.

Administratively, you oversee schedules, coordinate rehearsals, manage budgets, communicate with church leadership, resolve conflicts, and ensure that all the practical details are handled. You're also a teacher and mentor, developing the gifts of those you lead. This multifaceted role requires wisdom, humility, and dependence on God's strength. You cannot do it alone, which is why surrounding yourself with capable leaders is essential.

THE ROLE OF CHOIR OFFICERS

Choir officers serve as your leadership team, helping to carry the weight of ministry responsibilities. These may include a president who helps with overall coordination, a secretary who manages communication and documentation, a treasurer who handles financial matters, and section leaders who oversee specific vocal parts.

Officers should be selected not just for their musical ability but for their spiritual maturity, reliability, and heart for service. Invest time in training and empowering your officers. Meet with them regularly to plan, problem-solve, and pray. When your officers are strong, your entire ministry becomes stronger.

THE ROLE OF VOLUNTEERS IN ADMINISTRATION

Beyond formal officers, there are numerous administrative tasks that volunteers can handle: organizing music libraries, managing sound equipment, coordinating transportation for events, handling hospitality, maintaining social media presence, and countless other details that keep a ministry running smoothly.

Identify people with administrative gifts and invite them to serve in these capacities. Many people in your congregation have professional skills in organization, communication, or technology that could bless your ministry tremendously. Don't assume they need to sing or play an instrument to contribute meaningfully to your music ministry.

THE ROLE OF THE CHOIR MEMBER

Every choir member has a vital role to play. Beyond showing up and singing, choir members are ministers who carry responsibility for their own spiritual preparation, faithful attendance, positive attitude, and supportive presence within the group. They are representatives of the ministry both on and off the platform.

Help your choir members understand that they're not performers but worshipers, not audience entertainers but fellow servants. When each member takes ownership of their role and contribution, the entire ministry elevates. Communicate clear expectations while also celebrating the unique ways each person adds value to the whole.

MAINTAINING YOUR MUSIC MINISTRY

Building a ministry is one thing; maintaining it over the long haul is another challenge entirely. It's a pattern we see repeatedly: excitement runs high at the beginning of something fresh and new, but it doesn't take long for the initial hype to fade away. How do we keep our music ministry engaged, growing, and effective year after year?

Consider the Ministry on a Weekly Basis

Maintenance requires consistent attention. You cannot put your music ministry on autopilot and expect it to thrive. Make it a practice to think about your ministry weekly. Ask yourself: What went well? What needs improvement? Who needs encouragement? What upcoming needs should we prepare for? Are we still aligned with our vision?

This weekly reflection allows you to address small issues before they become big problems and to consistently shepherd your people rather than managing crises. It keeps you proactive rather than reactive.

Plan Outings, Retreats, and Concerts

Ministry cannot only happen within the four walls of rehearsal and Sunday services. People need variety, fun, and opportunities to bond outside of formal ministry settings. Plan regular outings where your choir can simply enjoy fellowship—perhaps a dinner, a movie night, a game night, or a seasonal outing. These informal gatherings build relationships and create the relational glue that holds a ministry together through challenging times.

Retreats serve a different but equally important purpose. A retreat provides extended time for spiritual refreshment, musical preparation, vision casting, and deeper relationship building. Even a simple overnight or day-long retreat can renew your team's sense of purpose and unity.

Concerts and special events give your ministry something to work toward and create opportunities to minister beyond your regular congregation. Whether it's an annual concert, participation in a community event, or a special service, these events provide focus, challenge your team to grow, and expand your ministry's impact.

Your Choir Members Matter

Never forget that you're leading people, not just producing music. Each person in your ministry has a story, struggles, dreams, and needs. They need to know they matter—not just for what they contribute but for who they are. Learn their names, remember details about their lives, celebrate their birthdays and milestones, pray for them specifically, and check in when they're absent.

Create a culture where people genuinely care for one another. Encourage your members to support each other during difficult times and rejoice together in victories. When people feel valued and connected, they remain committed even through seasons when participation feels more like discipline than delight.

Invest in Professional Development

As the leader, your growth directly impacts your ministry's growth. You cannot give what you don't have, and you cannot lead where you haven't gone. Make it a priority to attend professional development conferences, workshops, and retreats designed for worship leaders and music ministers. These experiences refresh your vision, expand your skills, expose you to new music and methods, and connect you with fellow ministers who understand your unique challenges.

Don't view professional development as a luxury or self-indulgence—it's an investment in your ministry's future. When you return with fresh inspiration, new music, and practical ideas, your entire ministry benefits. You'll avoid stagnation, stay current with trends in worship, and model the principle of lifelong learning for those you lead.

MOVING FORWARD

Building and maintaining an effective music and arts ministry is both an art and a calling. It requires clear vision, solid structure, consistent attention, and a heart that genuinely loves God and people. There will be seasons of great momentum and seasons of challenge. There will be victories to celebrate and obstacles to overcome. Through it all, remember your intention, return to your vision, and trust that God will be faithful to complete the work He has started through you.

Your ministry may never look like anyone else's, and that's perfectly fine. God has given you a unique assignment in a unique context. Effectiveness isn't about comparison or imitation—it's about faithfully stewarding what God has entrusted to you and watching Him bring forth fruit that glorifies His name and blesses His people.

As you apply these principles, pray continually, lead humbly, and serve wholeheartedly. The harvest you'll reap—transformed lives, deepened faith, and worship that truly honors God—will far exceed any temporary challenges you face along the way.

ABOUT THE AUTHOR

Dr. Will Harris is a renowned singer, songwriter, musician, recording artist, and author. A native of Oxford, Mississippi, Harris began playing piano and singing in church at an early age and assumed his first Minister of Music role at just fourteen.

Dr. Harris currently serves as the Director of Music and Fine Arts at the Historic Metropolitan Baptist Church in Washington, DC.

In 2013, Harris founded his award-winning recording choir, "Will Harris and Friends"—a global music ministry comprised of music educators, worship leaders, and psalmists from Fayetteville, North Carolina, as well as singers from across the United States.

Will Harris has composed and performed nationally and internationally with The Gospel Music Workshop of America and the National Convention of Gospel Choirs and Choruses. He is a multi-award-winning gospel recording artist and the 2022 Dunamis Gospel Award Music of Excellence Recipient. Harris has also performed in several musicals, including *The Color Purple*, *Jelly's Last Jam*, and *Lilies of the Field*.

Harris holds a bachelor's degree in vocal music from Rust College, a master's degree in education from the University of Phoenix, a Certificate of Worship from the Robert Webber Institute for Worship Studies, and an honorary doctorate from the School of the Great Commission Theological Seminary.

Dr. Harris is the author of his autobiography, *Taylor Made*—a narrative crafted with resilience and dedicated to dreamers everywhere who strive to make their visions a reality. *Taylor Made* is available for purchase through Barnes & Noble, Amazon, or by visiting www.willharrismusic.com.

ALSO BY DR. WILL HARRIS

Taylor Made: My Life, My Story

www.ingramcontent.com/pod-product-compliance
Ingram Content Group UK Ltd.
Pitfield, Milton Keynes, MK11 3LW, UK
UKHW020422250726
13967UKWH00007B/2766

9 781961 475724